DATE DUE

JAN 17 1995		DEC 16 1994	

THE DIVORCE ISSUE
AND REFORM IN
NINETEENTH-CENTURY
INDIANA

Richard Wires

BALL STATE MONOGRAPH NUMBER EIGHT

NOT FOR SALE

The Divorce Issue and Reform in Nineteenth-Century Indiana

Richard Wires

Associate Professor of History
Ball State University

Indiana. Ball State University, Muncie.
Ball state Monograph.)

Indiana. Ball state University, Muncie.
Publications in ~~English~~ History.)

BALL STATE MONOGRAPH NUMBER EIGHT

Publications in History, No. 2

Ball State University, Muncie, Indiana

1967

Preface

The path to awareness of the circumstances reported in this brief study was indirect. It began with research on the adventurous career of German archaeologist Heinrich Schliemann, famed excavator of the Homeric sites of early Greek civilization, who appeared rather mysteriously in Indiana to secure a divorce in 1869. A quest for the explanation of his action led to both discoveries and difficulties, for the general situation regarding divorce in Indiana became quite obvious, but there was seemingly no available analysis of the exact nature and development of the question. It appeared that the problem merited attention. The first product of subsequent research endeavors was the publication of an article dealing with a limited phase of the controversy. In the present study a more comprehensive treatment of the subject has been attempted. Award of a research grant from Ball State University has helped to make the investigations possible.

Emphasis of approach in this monograph has been placed on the legal and legislative aspects of the divorce issue and reform. No substantial effort has been directed toward analysis of either statistical data or public opinion. The readily obtainable figures do not permit precise or exhaustive study: often the statistics are available only for specified periods of time, rather than in annual computations, and with time segments chosen for different purposes being dissimilar. Under such circumstances it is possible to grasp general patterns only. Thus, the principal reason for presenting such data in the study is to indicate the relative seriousness of the divorce question. Use of public opinion indicators has been restricted to a few references in order to convey the approximate extent and tone of the controversy. The study is, therefore, essentially one centered on legal principles and legislative procedures involved in the process of securing divorce reform.

Suggestions of great value have been offered by friends and associates at various stages in the preparation of the

iii

manuscript. Lois Hartley of Boston College and Robert Evans of Ball State University were extremely helpful in matters of style and usage; Roy Gruenewald, Herbert Hamilton, and Bert Anson gave me the benefit of their special knowledge and experience; and Morton Rosenberg's advice was a welcome assistance throughout the long process of research and writing. To all of them I am grateful and indebted for their time and comments. Yet responsibility for the form and substance of the final product must remain exclusively my own. Much of the task of typing the manuscript was borne with customary patience and skill by Linda Anderson. A last acknowledgment must be reserved for Gertrude Kane and her staff for their invaluable aid in taking the publication through the necessary processes.

R. W.

Table of Contents

Divorce in American and Indiana Law_____ 2

Incidence of Divorce as a Source of Controversy_____ 6

Criticisms of Provisions and Procedures_____ 10

Public Reaction to the Indiana Situation_____ 17

Reform Efforts before the Civil War_____ 19

The Divorce Law of 1873_____ 25

Effects of Reform _____ 31

List of Tables

I.   Divorces in the U.S. by Year, 1860-1873_____ 7

II. Divorces in the U.S. by State, 1867-1881_____ 8

III. Populations of Relevant States, 1860-1880_____ 8

IV. Indiana Counties Granting 100 or More Divorces in
     Quinary Periods, 1867-1881, and Populations_____ 9

V.   Divorces in the U.S., 1867-1880, and in Indiana,
     1867-1881, in Percentages by Cause and Party_____ 12

The Divorce Issue and Reform
in Nineteenth-Century Indiana

During the middle years of the nineteenth century, Indiana found itself the center of a major controversy over the nature and administration of its divorce law. In an era when divorce was neither socially accepted nor statistically common in American life, Indiana not only operated under a divorce statute that was extremely liberal in its general content, but the state's courts too frequently displayed a procedural laxity that further eased the procurement of divorces. The situation soon aroused considerable indignation. Especially objectionable to many observers was the fact that combined legal and judicial circumstances made it possible for residents of other states to secure divorces in Indiana with little difficulty. Public reaction to migratory divorce-seekers and places that accommodated them was even stronger a century ago than it appears to be today. Although awareness of the problem stirred a modest reform movement in Indiana during the late 1850's, the principal reasons for the criticism remained unchanged through the Civil War period, and the various forms of protest against the state were consequently renewed in the postwar years. Only by elimination of the main sources of contention from its divorce law in 1873, and with greater insistence by its courts upon honest representation of facts, was Indiana able to silence the numerous critics of its divorce law and procedures. Yet for more than two decades the state possessed an unenviable reputation as a jurisdiction of easy and ready divorce.

Understanding of the controversy in its wider scope necessarily involves consideration of two closely interrelated factors. One was the idea of divorce in any form or under any circumstances. The very concept was objectionable to many Americans for religious and social reasons. Since Indiana had already long accepted divorce in principle, and was further prepared to permit its citizens substantial latitude in the entire question, it was inevitably censured for permitting dissolution of marriages. But Indiana remained generally disinclined to heed this type of broad criticism. Its legal sovereignty allowed it to determine its own policy with respect to marital status and family affairs. This right was firmly upheld by both leaders and people.

More difficult to counter was the charge that abuses in execution of the Indiana law allowed residents of other states to obtain divorces in Indiana that would perhaps not have been permitted in their own jurisdictions. Although the issue of recognition of out-of-state divorces under the "full faith and credit" provision of the federal Constitution was still nascent a century ago, the implications of the situation were certainly seen by contemporary observers, and the notoriety that attached to some divorces under the Indiana law produced an understandably loud outcry from the officials and public in other states. Indiana did not deny the existence of specific injustices under its divorce law but was reluctant to acknowledge the necessity for thorough reform. There appears to have been at first a widespread conviction that individual courts could prevent unsatisfactory situations without resort to major change in the law. Then preoccupation with the more pressing problems of the Civil War decade, especially as they affected the political functioning of the postwar legislature sessions, added notably to the postponement of any real solution to the less important divorce question. But increasing public uneasiness about the problem and its serious consequences eventually produced the 1873 reform.

Six fundamental elements warrant analysis in connection with the divorce issue in Indiana: the principles of divorce law in American and Indiana jurisprudence, the actual frequency of divorce in Indiana during the period, the sources of controversy under the Indiana statute and procedures, the nature of the public reaction in Indiana and elsewhere to the situation, the unsuccessful attempts at reform before the Civil War, and the correction of abuses in the system by legislation in 1873. Examination of these topics will place the entire problem in its proper legal and statistical perspective, clarify the specific aspects and practices most in contention, and show the difficulties encountered in the process of securing a better law of divorce.

Divorce in American and Indiana Law

In the United States, marriage has been regarded as a civil contract, but dissolution of it cannot be effected at the pleasure of the parties. The state as the representative of society in general is an interested third party in the marriage relationship and termination of a marriage is therefore officially recognized only when the legal processes have been followed. Under our federal system matters relating to marriage are left to state regulation, but the attitudes of the various states have never been uniform. Three concepts have generally been accepted. Annulment merely invalidates or nullifies a marriage which is for some cause deemed voidable. Divorce dissolves an admittedly valid marriage contract. Two types of divorce have been common: an absolute and complete dissolution (divorce *a vinculo matrimonii*) and a limited dissolution or legal separation from bed and board (divorce *a mensa et thoro*). In the latter instance remarriage is not possible. The method of obtaining a divorce has also varied among the states. Some have specified that divorces could be granted legislatively, by special acts of law to affect stipulated individual cases, while others have allowed only judicial divorces following court hearings. Grounds for divorce have likewise shown little consistency in the separate jurisdictions. Each state has determined what circumstances would justify termination of a marriage. The statutes and rulings that result from these diversities of outlook have long created serious problems in respect to American divorce law. A century ago the situation was already a point of contention.

Before 1851 it was possible in Indiana to obtain a divorce through either legislative or judicial action. A special act of the state legislature could dissolve a specific marriage, and the method appears to have been used rather frequently. For example, one index cites a total of 104 legislative divorces from 1807 through 1846, with 41 of them occurring among the local acts of 1846.[1] Such a procedure must certainly have been an increasingly burdensome task when the legislature had more important business to transact. Judicial divorces were also made available. In 1824 Indiana already had a law permitting circuit courts to grant divorces on several grounds.[2] The law was reenacted in 1831[3] and again in 1843 without major substantive change. An attempt was made in the Revised Statutes of 1843 to integrate all matters of domestic relations into one comprehensive law. Hence the divorce provisions formed Article II of the law, comprising Sections 22 through 72, and were much more detailed than earlier or later divorce laws.[4] The last section declared that

---

[1] George Pence, *Index of Indiana Laws* (Private, 1921), IV, pages not numbered.
[2] *The Revised Laws of Indiana* (1824), 156-157.
[3] *Ibid.* (1831), 213-215.
[4] *The Revised Statutes of Indiana* (1843), 598-606.

"no divorce *a mensa et thoro* shall be granted by the courts of this state," but such limited decrees had apparently never been very common in Indiana. Together these laws set the pattern, hereafter discussed, of the Indiana divorce legislation.

The matter of divorce regulation was raised when the new Constitution was being drafted in 1850-1851, but the only concept to receive serious attention was a prohibition of legislative divorces. Most of the proposals concerning divorce were therefore joined with items describing types of powers to be denied to the legislative branch. Soon after the delegates had assembled in October, 1850, a resolution was introduced to prevent the legislature from granting divorces.[5] It was subsequently referred to the Committee on the Legislative Department of Government, which included it in tentative wording of Article XII, Section 28: the General Assembly "shall have no power to grant divorces" or direct by law the sale of estates belonging to infants or others under legal disability, "but by general law, shall confer such favor on the courts of justice."[6] This item was approved for adoption before Christmas and sent to the Committee on Arrangement and Phraseology.[7] Also under consideration by the committee was a draft version of Article XXXV, Section 1, which also specified that legislative divorces were among those types of local or special laws to be prohibited. In its report early in February, 1851, the committee combined the two references into Article II, Section 22, with the wording that was eventually incorporated into the final document as Article IV, Section 22, declaring that "The General Assembly shall not pass local or special laws, in any of the following enumerated cases, that is to say: . . . Granting divorces . . ."[8] In the text of their address to the people on the new Constitution, the delegates to the Convention pointed out that among the twelve provisions "tending to check and regulate the Legislative branch of government" not found in the old Constitution was the prohibition of legislative divorces.[9]

With adoption of the new fundamental law giving exclusive competence in divorce matters to the courts, the question of statutory requirements and regulations for divorce procedures was again

[5] *Journal of the Convention of the People of the State of Indiana, to Amend the Constitution, Assembled at Indianapolis, October 1850* (Indianapolis, 1851), 26, and *Report of the Debates and Proceedings of the Convention for the Revision of the Constitution of the State of Indiana, 1850* (Indianapolis, 1850), 40. Titles are hereafter abbreviated.
[6] *Debates of the Convention,* 58, and *Journal of the Convention,* 169-170.
[7] *Debates of the Convention,* 1274, 1279, and *Journal of the Convention,* 506, 514.
[8] *Journal of the Convention,* 926-934.
[9] *Ibid.,* 967.

raised. It appears that Robert Dale Owen exercised substantial influence in shaping Indiana's divorce law by endorsing its basic principles on several occasions, but later opinions that he was largely responsible for the law cannot be factually justified. Although Owen had approved the addition earlier of habitual drunkenness to the recognized grounds for divorce, he believed in 1852 that the existing provisions were essentially sound and workable, so he resisted efforts to change the law when it was re-examined. In referring to the action of the first legislative session after the Constitutional Convention, Owen observed that Indiana "merely reenacted the old divorce law."[10] The statute of May 13, 1852, was indeed only a simplified restatement of the old law, and it therefore easily passed both houses without real debate.[11] Although the law of 1852 was amended somewhat on March 4, 1859, it remained in force until its repeal in 1873, when a new statute was promulgated eliminating features that had become controversial. Because the law of 1852 was basically the same as earlier statutes, it has been taken as the most convenient point of departure for this study.[12] Moreover, not until after 1852 was there any extensive social or legal problem connected with divorce in Indiana. Hence, the two decades from 1852 to 1873 comprise the years most noteworthy in respect to the divorce issue in Indiana.

Widespread attention was drawn to Indiana's divorce law and procedures for several closely related but separable reasons, and for purposes of detailed introduction it is possible to organize the discussion according to those critical issues. Perhaps most essential to an appreciation of the entire problem is an analysis of the relatively high incidence of divorce in Indiana. A twofold purpose will thus be served: to illustrate that divorce in general was not a common occurrence in the United States and to compare the available figures for the nation as a whole with those for Indiana and other individual states. Then it is necessary to examine the two principal factors contributing to the Indiana divorce rate. One such cause was recognition in Indiana of grounds for divorce that were unusually liberal for the times, and the other was an ease in acquiring or alleg-

---

[10] Statements by Owen in *The Tribune* (New York), March 5, 1860, reprinted in Horace Greeley, *Recollections of a Busy Life* (New York, 1869), 573-578.

[11] *Journal of the House of Representatives* (1851), II, 1315-1316, 1331-1332, 1472-1473; *Journal of the Senate* (1851), 902, 908, 932.

[12] The text of the 1852 law appears in the *Revised Statutes* (1852), II, 233-238, and in the *Statutes of 1852*, Gavin and Hord Edition, 348-354. An excellent discussion of the early Indiana divorce regulations is contained in the Indiana Supreme Court's opinion in Tolen v. Tolen, 2 Blackford 407 (1831).

ing residence that made the state a convenient jurisdiction in the early migratory divorce market. Together these elements brought criticism of the Indiana law and consequently demands for revision of its provisions. Each source of controversy will therefore be treated separately as it existed under the 1852 law before chronological presentation of the efforts to amend the law and correct the weaknesses in it is made.

Incidence of Divorce as a Source of Controversy

A question that must inevitably be resolved in consideration of divorce reform is the actual frequency of divorces. To those who oppose all divorce on moral or religious grounds, any decree may be deemed improper; to those who accept the concept of divorce, the issue generally centers about the relative liberality of the laws and courts; to those who find the nature and use of divorce noncontroversial, a high frequency of it is seldom disturbing. A century ago the inherent idea of divorce was much debated and the frequency of it much deplored. Yet available statistics indicate that divorce was not especially common in the United States. Certain areas were known for comparative leniency, however, and Indiana as such a jurisdiction was criticized widely. The following paragraphs present the situation factually at relevant national, state, and county levels in order to illustrate the problem and perspective of the time.

Throughout the period under consideration there was a slow rise in the divorce rate in the United States, with a slight drop during the early Civil War years and a temporary increase in the immediate postwar months, but the change was paralleled by growth in the national population and the number of existing marriages. Table I presents the pertinent figures. The divorce rate per 1,000 people remained virtually constant at .3, except when the Civil War curtailed the procurement of decrees, because of general population expansion. Later the rate rose sharply to .7 divorces per 1,000 population in 1898, 1.0 by 1911, 2.0 by 1940, and 3.5 by the end of World War II.[13] Similarly, the number of annual marriages rose from an estimated 256,000 in 1860 to an officially tabulated 386,000 in 1873. Since there was a decrease in marriages during the Civil War and a

---

[13] Bureau of the Census, *Historical Statistics of the United States, 1789-1945: A Supplement to the Statistical Abstract of the United States* (Washington, 949), 49.

6

TABLE I

DIVORCES IN THE U.S. BY YEAR, 1860-1873[14]

Year	Total Number of Divorces	Divorces per 1,000 Total Population	Divorces per 1,000 Existing Marriages
1860	7,380	.3	1.2
1861	6,540	.2	1.1
1862	6,230	.2	1.0
1863	6,760	.2	1.1
1864	8,940	.3	1.4
1865	10,090	.3	1.6
1866	11,530	.3	1.8
1867	9,937	.3	1.5
1868	10,150	.3	1.5
1869	10,939	.3	1.6
1870	10,962	.3	1.5
1871	11,586	.3	1.6
1872	12,390	.3	1.7
1873	13,156	.3	1.7

sharp increase after the conflict, national divorce and marriage rates tended to decline and accelerate simultaneously, bringing only a slight overall rise in divorces per 1,000 existing marriages. For purposes of further comparison that rate jumped from 1.7 in 1873 to 2.0 in 1879, then to 4.0 in 1900, and has been over 9.0 since 1941.[15] In view of these figures it can hardly be asserted that the number of divorces in the United States as a whole constituted a serious social or legal problem. But analysis by the several states offers a better picture of the prevailing situation.

Extensive statistical data on marriage and divorce were first compiled by the Bureau of the Census in 1867, and the figures reveal that in the following years three midwestern states led the nation in granting divorces. Of 328,716 divorces decreed in the United States from 1867 through 1886, the courts of Illinois allowed 36,072; Ohio, 26,367; and Indiana, 25,193.[16] Table II breaks down the first fifteen years of that period into quinary segments and shows that Illinois always permitted the most divorces. During the first five years the number of decrees in Indiana almost equalled the

[14] Data presented in Table I are a composite of figures taken from Table 42, "Number of Absolute Divorces and Annulments, and Rates, United States, 1860-1956," and Table 70, "Marital Dissolutions by Death and Divorce per 1,000 Existing Marriages, and Per Cent of Dissolutions by Divorce, U.S., 1860-1956," in Paul H. and Pauline F. Jacobson, *American Marriage and Divorce* (New York, 1959), 90, 142. The figures combine divorce, annulment, and legal separation decrees; the rate computions exclude the slave population prior to 1865.

[15] *Ibid.*, 21-22, 91-92, 141-142.

[16] Bureau of the Census, *Marriage and Divorce, 1867-1906; Part II, General Tables* (Washington, 1908), 4.

Illinois total, but Indiana fell to third place behind Ohio in the subsequent five-year periods. Such figures assume much greater significance, however, when compared with state populations set forth in Table III. Since Indiana was the least populous of the states concerned, its proportional divorce rate was considerably higher,

TABLE II

DIVORCES IN THE U.S. BY STATE, 1867-1881[17]

Period	Total Divorces in U.S.	Illinois	Indiana	Ohio	Other States
1867-1871	53,574	5,803	5,741	4,729	None over 4,000
1872-1876	68,547	8,516	5,089	5,611	None over 4,000
1877-1881	89,284	9,702	6,523	7,093	Michigan 5,492; no others over 5,000

TABLE III

POPULATIONS OF RELEVANT STATES, 1860-1880[18]

Year	Illinois	Indiana	Ohio	Michigan
1860	1,711,951	1,350,428	2,339,511	749,113
1870	2,539,891	1,680,637	2,665,260	1,184,059
1880	3,077,871	1,978,301	3,198,062	1,636,937

especially during the years before 1873. In the period 1867-1871 the nearly similar divorce totals in Illinois and Indiana represented in each instance more than ten per cent of the total divorces in the entire nation. When it is realized that in 1870 Illinois had over 850,-000 more people than Indiana, a number that meant Indiana possessed about two-thirds as many inhabitants as its western neighbor, it becomes readily apparent that Indiana's ratio of divorces to population was substantially higher. The following period was somewhat less notable, for Indiana was third in total divorces and even granted fewer than earlier, but in ratio of divorces to population Indiana surpassed Ohio and followed Illinois. A rapid rise in the number of decrees granted in Indiana during the 1877-1881 period brought a

---

[17] *Ibid.*
[18] U.S. Census Office, *Compendium of the Tenth Census (June 1, 1880)* (Washington, 1883), I, 24, 25, 35, 46.

8

comparable result. The state was third in total divorces granted but second in ratio of divorces to population. Michigan, with fewer people and a growing number of divorces, led. Illinois and Ohio were third and fourth, respectively, because of far greater populations. As divorces become more common in the United States, the significance of Indiana in the divorce statistics decreased substantially.

Table IV indicates the Indiana counties that granted more than 100 divorces in the selected five-year periods and the populations of those counties in 1870 and 1880. On the basis of actual numbers

TABLE IV

INDIANA COUNTIES GRANTING 100 OR MORE DIVORCES
IN QUINARY PERIODS, 1867-1881, AND POPULATIONS[19]

County	Population 1870	Divorces 1867-1871	Divorces 1872-1876	Divorces 1877-1881	Population 1880
Allen	43,494	403	254	266	54,763
Clark	24,770			109	28,610
DeKalb	17,167	132		114	20,225
Delaware	19,030			102	22,926
Elkhart	26,026	216	124	138	33,454
Floyd	23,300	107		111	24,590
Jackson	18,974			103	23,050
Marion	71,939	366	661	697	102,782
Montgomery	23,765			100	27,316
Noble	20,389	144		133	22,956
Posey	19,185			109	20,857
St. Joseph	25,322	123		127	33,178
Steuben	12,854	121			14,645
Tippecanoe	33,515	135	147	153	35,966
Vanderburgh	33,145	163	175	264	42,193
Vigo	33,549	322	322	330	45,658
State	1,680,637	5,741	5,089	6,523	1,978,301

of decrees the five counties in 1867-1871 that ranked highest were Allen, Marion, Vigo, Elkhart, and Vanderburgh. When the 1870 population of the counties is compared to their decrees of divorce, however, it appears that Allen, DeKalb, Elkhart, Steuben, and Vigo counties (not ranked) had relatively high ratios of divorces to inhabitants. Also significant is the fact that the decrease in divorces in the state during the 1872-1876 period, when the tighter law of 1873 had become effective, is reflected in the fact that only six counties

[19] Based on population figures in U.S. Census Office, *A Compendium of the Ninth Census (June 1, 1870)* (Washington, 1872), 40-43, and *Compendium of the Tenth Census*, I, 25-27; and divorce statistics in *Marriage and Divorce, 1867-1906*, part II, 755-756. Madison County records, which were destroyed by fire in 1880, could not be included.

exceeded the arbitrarily chosen figure of 100 divorces. Eleven counties had previously been in that category. The 1877-1881 period shows an increase in total divorces in the state with Marion, Vigo, Allen, Vanderburgh, and Tippecanoe counties leading in the number of decrees. But greater populations and substantially fewer divorces in many counties (Allen and Elkhart, for example, are noteworthy) account for a definite change in the pattern. Distribution of the decrees among the counties was wider, with fifteen counties granting more than 100 divorces, and with no county having the high ratio of divorces to population that occurred in some areas before 1873.

From the foregoing presentation of basic divorce statistics it is apparent that in the nation as a whole divorce did not constitute a major problem a century ago, especially in view of later national trends, but the very nature of divorce and even rather limited occurrences of it aroused considerable social concern. Particular attention was therefore focused on those jurisdictions where divorce was highest in actual numbers of decrees, most frequent in ratio to population, and easiest to obtain in respect to cause and procedure. Examination of the various figures shows that Indiana, adhering to a relatively liberal position on divorce at a time when it was neither fully accepted nor extremely common in the United States, was demonstrably open to criticism on such counts. For this reason the state was the object of undesired national publicity, and local sentiment demanded divorce reform to remove the stigma.

Criticisms of Provisions and Procedures

A primary source of argument always concerned the permissible grounds for divorce. Indiana allowed great latitude of cause from its earliest years and thereafter showed little inclination to alter its stand. In its first extensive treatment of divorce in the state, the Indiana Supreme Court in 1831 acknowledged the constitutionality of the seven prescribed grounds: (1) a former subsisting marriage, (2) impotency, (3) adultery, (4) abandonment, (5) condemnation for a felony, (6) barbarous and inhuman treatment, and (7) other reasonable and proper cause.[20] The first of those grounds was later dropped, because a bigamous marriage did not require legal dissolu-

---

[20] Tolen v. Tolen, 2 Blackford 407 (1831).

tion through divorce; and habitual drunkenness was subsequently added to the list. An attempt to include a provision in the 1851 Constitution that the legislature could never pass a law allowing divorces for any cause except fornication was a failure.[21] Thus, when the new divorce law was enacted in 1852, it embodied the same general grounds as previously accepted: (1) adultery, except where there was connivance, consent, or mutuality, (2) impotency, (3) "abandonment for one year, or for a less period if the court shall be satisfied that reconciliation is improbable," (4) cruel treatment, (5) habitual drunkenness of either party or failure of the husband to provide for the family, (6) conviction of an infamous crime, and (7) "any other cause for which the court shall deem it proper that the divorce shall be granted."[22]

Objections to the stipulated causes fell into three basic categories. Some continued to oppose on religious principles any ground but adultery; some sought to add or change periods of time during which the ground must have existed; and some wished to remove the court's discretion under the third, fourth, and seventh items. Divorces on the ground of desertion where a year's time had not yet lapsed were seemingly quite common, and cruel treatment was already construed liberally enough to include "simply incompatibility of temperament."[23] But in particular the seventh or "discretionary" clause caused difficulty. It had been a provision of the various laws for over twenty years, and its constitutionality had been affirmed in 1839. The test case concerned a man who had been fraudulently induced to marry a woman pregnant with another's child and who sued for divorce under the seventh clause because his predicament fitted no specific ground. The trial court dismissed his action on the basis that the discretionary clause gave the court unconstitutional legislative power. Upon appeal the provision was upheld by the state Supreme Court in an opinion that pointed out that allowing discretion in a court was not permitting it to legislate:

> Like all discretionary power in Courts, it must be exercised in a sound and legal manner; it must not be governed by caprice or prejudice, or wild and visionary notions with regard to the marriage institution, but should be so directed as to conduce to domestic harmony, and the peace and morality of society. It must be conformable to the common sense and feeling of the community. The application of such a standard to an alleged cause of divorce in a particular case, is not the enactment of a law.

---

[21] *Journal of the Convention*, 232.
[22] *Statutes of 1852*, Gavin and Hord Edition, 348-354, Sections 7 and 8.
[23] *Brevier Legislative Reports* (1873), 454.

11

Hence, the court ruled that the provision was constitutional but that a court's use of discretion was reviewable through appeal.[24] None of the other causes was challenged on legal grounds, but there continued to be legislative attempts to change them.

Table V offers a composite presentation of the grounds relied upon for divorce in the United States and Indiana from 1867 to 1881. Attention might first be directed to the figures indicating the party obtaining the decree. At the national level the percentage of divorces awarded wives remained between 64.0 and 66.1 during each period cited. Although the Indiana figures are not for the exact years, they are for approximately the same periods, at least sufficiently close for purposes of comparison. In the 1867-1871

TABLE V

Divorces in the U.S., 1867-1880, and in Indiana, 1867-1881, in Percentages by Cause and Party[25]

	UNITED STATES			INDIANA			
Cause	1867-1870	1871-1875	1876-1880		1867-1871	1872-1876	1877-1881
Adultery	26.4	21.5	19.3	H	8.9	7.5	8.4
				W	2.1	2.7	2.4
Cruelty	12.4	14.8	15.8	H	3.4	2.5	1.5
				W	8.9	10.5	12.0
Desertion	35.4	37.4	38.8	H	13.6	10.1	9.4
				W	15.6	16.6	17.6
Drunkenness	3.0	4.3	4.3	H	.2	.2	.2
				W	1.9	2.3	2.2
Neglect to Provide	1.6	2.0	2.4	H	.0	.0	.0
				W	4.9	5.5	6.3
Combinations	13.4	13.2	12.3	H	3.1	4.7	4.2
				W	20.3	25.7	28.3
All Others	7.8	6.8	7.1	H	5.6	3.3	2.0
				W	9.7	8.4	5.6
Party							
Husband	36.0	33.9	34.3		36.6	28.2	25.8
Wife	64.0	66.1	65.7		63.4	71.8	74.2

[24] Ritter v. Ritter, 5 Blackford 81 (1839).
[25] Compiled from material in Jacobson, 121, Table 58, "Per Cent of Absolute Divorces and Annulments by Party to Which Granted, and by Legal Ground, United States, 1867-1950"; *Marriage and Divorce, 1867-1906*, part II, 99-102, 553; and Alfred Cahen, *Statistical Analysis of American Divorce* (New York, 1932), 35. Computation of percentages from actual number of decrees in Indiana was done by this writer.

period 63.4 per cent of the decrees went to wives; the figure jumped to 71.8 per cent in 1872-1876; thereafter it rose again in 1877-1881 to 74.2 per cent. Only the percentage for the first five-year segment coincides roughly with the national figure, while the others show higher rates. This finding should not be overemphasized, however, because the figures available do not cover absolutely identical units. Yet it reflects a generally liberal atmosphere in the state concerning women's right to sue and a great readiness to allow wives relief against erring husbands.[26]

In the nation as a whole the individual causes that were most often given for procurement of divorces were desertion or abandonment, adultery, and cruelty. Other grounds, separately or in combination, were less common. The figures are primarily of importance for comparative purposes, for many states recognized only a few causes, thereby making impossible any accurate conclusions nationally. Adultery probably dropped as a stated cause, for example, because less notorious grounds could be used under liberalized laws. Some grounds listed in Table V were not widely accepted. In Indiana the same three specific grounds were most frequent, but their rank was desertion or abandonment, cruelty, and adultery. The reversal of position for cruelty and adultery from national figures arose most likely, as noted above, from the availability of causes that could be substituted in allegations for adultery. Jurisdictions that accepted no cause but adultery for divorce perhaps encouraged its use as a legal ground whenever couples agreed to separate and needed a recognized ground. Also noteworthy is the relatively high occurrence in Indiana of combined and miscellaneous causes. Impotency existed as a ground in Indiana and is not listed separately, but it could hardly have been a frequent cause of divorce. The most valid conclusion from the figures is that Indiana showed greater willingness to grant divorces where the facts taken as a whole seemed to warrant such remedy but divorce could perhaps not be factually justified under any particular ground. Undoubtedly many complaints relied upon the discretionary clause in the divorce statute, and, under that provision or for other reasons, the courts must have leaned toward the spirit rather than the letter of the law.

The most criticized provisions of the Indiana divorce law were those pertaining to residence requirements and service of summons.

---

[26] Section 16 of the 1852 law allowed a wife to sue for divorce in her own name upon proof of two years' maintenance of good reputation as to chastity and virtue. *Statutes of 1852*, Gavin and Hord Edition, 348-354.

13

In part the difficulty arose from the loose requirements of the law itself, and in part it stemmed from the failure of the courts to demand greater proof of residence. But the combined effect was to encourage residents of other states to come to Indiana, either establish a temporary residence or falsify such a residence, and obtain a divorce decree perhaps not otherwise available to them. Unquestionably the migratory divorce market accounts for the relatively high rate of divorce in Indiana. Ease in fulfilling in some manner the state's residence obligations and ability to meet one of the state's liberal grounds for divorce brought upon Indiana the charge of being a national haven for divorce-seekers from stricter jurisdictions.

Under the 1852 law the procedure to obtain a divorce was quite simple.[27] Section 6 provided that a petitioner need not have been a resident of the state for any prescribed length of time but need only have been at the moment a *bona fide* resident of the county in which he filed his suit.[28] And his own affidavit of such residence was designated by the statute as *prima facie* evidence. Thus each person determined for himself, unless challenged, the status of his residence. Once the petition was filed, service of the summons was made by the clerk of the court. Where the defendant was a resident of Indiana, Section 10 required service to be personal, by reading it to the defendant or by leaving a copy at his usual place of residence, but cases involving resident defendants created few problems. If it appeared "by the affidavit of a disinterested person" or by the return of the summons officer that the defendant was not an Indiana resident, the statute in Section 11 provided for constructive or legal notice, whereby "publication for three successive weeks in some weekly newspaper of general circulation" in the county of suit (or nearest Indiana county with a newspaper) was deemed sufficient. The chance of a nonresident defendant learning of the pending divorce suit through notice published in local Indiana newspapers was obviously extremely negligible. Fourteen days after personal service or thirty days after publication notice was made, the court under Section 12 might proceed to hear and determine the case. Section 13 required proof of the allegations even if the defendant failed to appear, and Section 27 stated that the public prosecutor was to oppose the petition in the defendant's absence; the former requirement was easily

---

[27] *Ibid.*

[28] The law of 1824 required only residence in the county at the time of filing suit; under the 1831 law twelve months' state residence was required; and in 1843 the state residence was raised to two years' duration.

overcome and the latter stipulation proved ineffective. A defendant was permitted under Section 14 to file a cross-petition as well as an answer, so that the court could grant the decree to either party entitled to it, but judicial interpretation for a long time complicated this point.

The complex situations and legal problems that developed under the Indiana law are best explained by citation of actual cases that became decisive. Earliest of the significant court pronouncements on divorce in Indiana was the Tolen case of 1831. There the marriage had been performed in Kentucky, and the husband had abandoned his wife to live with another woman in that state. Later the wife moved to Indiana, where she acquired a *bona fide* residence, and filed suit for divorce. Since the husband had never lived in Indiana, he was notified by publication of the suit. Upon trial the lower court decided it had no jurisdiction because the marriage and alleged ground for divorce both occurred out of the state. The Indiana Supreme Court concluded that the court erred because it had power to hear the case. After a discussion of European and American legal opinions on divorce jurisdiction, the court held that a marriage contract is governed by the *lex domicilii*. Hence, "the laws of the country wherever the parties may be domiciled must be applied to their domestic relations." Referring to the Indiana provisions, the tribunal declared that it had "no doubt" the statute was constitutional.[29] Under this decision a party resident in Indiana could therefore file suit against a nonresident defendant. The ground cited for the petitioner's relief through divorce need not have taken place in Indiana. In 1858 the state Supreme Court affirmed its earlier holding in a case where the cause occurred entirely in New York State.[30]

Attempts were also made to test the constitutionality of the provisions for service or notice. But the Supreme Court had already held that notice by publication to nonresident defendants was enough where the petitioner was a resident of Indiana. In instances where the defendant later learned of the decree, the courts refused to open or set aside divorces on the basis of public policy. Frequently the party obtaining the decree had remarried, and the social evil of upsetting divorces and marriages was greater than any injustice done to the divorced spouse. The state's highest court had so ruled before

[29] Tolen v. Tolen, 2 Blackford 407 (1831). See especially 409-412.
[30] Wilcox v. Wilcox, 10 Ind. 436 (1858).

15

the 1852 law[31] and continued to adhere firmly to its position. When a nonresident husband who had been divorced on publication notice attempted to open the decree by assigning as error the failure of the prosecuting attorney to defend in his own absence (under Section 27 of the law), the court declared that there was no error because the official was merely obliged but not required to be present and his nonappearance did not prevent the court from proceeding.[32]

Such cases continued to cause serious difficulties, but the court always refused to open divorce decrees. The 1859 case of McQuigg v. McQuigg is an outstanding example. In 1854 the husband had obtained a divorce in Marion County, and in 1857 the wife sought to have the decree declared void. Both parties were residents of New York. The wife contended that her husband had never been a *bona fide* resident of Indiana and had obtained his divorce by fraud upon the court. Since the evidence of the husband's falsification of facts was quite clear, the lower court vacated the divorce judgment. McQuigg had subsequently remarried and was understandably very worried. But the Supreme Court reversed the lower court, citing its earlier decisions, and reiterated that "the policy of our state seems to have been, and to still be, against disturbing divorces granted." The case is particularly significant because (1) the verbatim account of the wife's legal arguments shows that her attorneys raised every important point in her favor, and (2) the evidence of fraud was incontrovertible. McQuigg filed for divorce on January 4, 1854, and got the decree on May 14, 1854. He had always kept his New York residence and business, had publicly announced his intention to return there after getting an Indiana divorce, and did in fact go back to New York with his new decree. Thus, the whole issue was whether deliberate falsification of residence still entitled a party to a valid divorce from the court. The attorneys for the wife declared that principle rather than personal rights was at stake:

> And the settlement of the case in accordance with principle, will certainly convey a salutary lesson to that large class of discontented or lecherous pilgrims seeking the *Mecca* of divorce, who turn their faces towards *Indiana,* as the happy region where the judgment they wish can be obtained the most easily and the most cheaply. It will secure private rights, by vindicating the purity of public justice.

---

[31] McJunkin v. McJunkin, 3 Ind. 30 (1851). Section 66 of the 1843 divorce law did stipulate that a court could "revoke all decrees and orders of divorce" not affecting third parties if a divorced couple remarried each other.

[32] Green v. Green, 7 Ind. 113 (1855). The provision was retained in the 1873 law as Section 26 but was of limited value under this interpretation.

16

Still, the Supreme Court realized the chaos that would result from the opening or voiding of court decrees in divorce and refused to allow the vacation of the decree even in face of extraordinary evidence of fraud by the petitioner.[33] The McQuigg decision was affirmed in 1860 after the amendments of 1859 incorporated the court's position.[34] Other states could of course refuse to recognize the validity of Indiana divorces where they decided the applicant was not a *bona fide* Indiana resident. But such rulings merely contributed to the confusion surrounding the status of the parties involved.

Public Reaction to the Indiana Situation

An indication of the national publicity given Indiana divorces was a newspaper debate in 1860 between Horace Greeley and Robert Dale Owen. In an editorial in *The New York Daily Tribune* of March 1, 1860, Greeley expressed his opposition to proposed changes in the New York divorce law that would have allowed divorces on grounds other than adultery. To warn his readers of the danger of liberal divorce laws he commented that

> The paradise of free-lovers is the State of Indiana, where the lax principles of Robert Dale Owen and the utter want of principle of John Pettit (leading revisers of the laws), combined to establish, some years since, a state of law which enables men or women to get unmarried nearly at pleasure.

Greeley then cited two examples of Indiana procedures. First he quoted a legal friend in Indiana who had told him he had obtained eleven divorces one morning before lunch "and it wasn't a good morning for divorces either." Then he mentioned the case of an Easterner who had journeyed to Indiana with his paramour, obtained a divorce, married his companion, returned to the East, and ordered his ex-wife to move out of the house. Greeley foresaw similar conditions in New York if the state law were changed.[35]

---

[33] McQuigg v. McQuigg, 13 Ind. 294 (1859). The court's opinion on 294-296 is followed by an abstract of the husband's argument against upsetting the decree, 296-298, and a reprint of the entire appellate argument of the wife's attorneys, 298-317. The long quotation is found on 313.

[34] Hoffman v. Hoffman, 15 Ind. 278 (1860).

[35] The texts of all the Greeley-Owen exchanges are reprinted from *The Tribune* in Greeley, 571-618, as "A Discussion with Robert Dale Owen of the Law of Divorce." Greeley's initial editorial is found on 571-573. A full analysis of the debate based on the original *Tribune* texts has been published: see Richard Wires, "The Greeley-Owen Divorce Debate of 1860," *Forum*, III (Spring 1962), 49-60.

17

Owen had returned to America in 1858 from his position as Minister at Naples and reacted strongly when he read the Greeley editorial. In his response, printed on March 5, he declared that the Indiana law owed nothing to Pettit but that he himself had always considered it a sound law for Indiana residents and had refused to alter it even when he had been in a position to advocate changes. He pointed out to Greeley, however, that the 1859 amendments made Indiana divorces harder for nonresidents to obtain. Then Owen retaliated in kind by observing that "It is in New York and New England, refusing reasonable divorce, that free-love prevails; not in Indiana. I never even heard the name there. You locate the Paradise, then, too far west." And he added that "For the rest, divorces in Indiana are far less frequent than strangers, reading our divorce law, might be led to imagine."[36] The controversy thereafter broadened into a general and hot dispute on religion, marriage, and divorce and continued through five exchanges in the columns of *The Tribune* during March and April.[37] Some of the points raised by the men were of questionable accuracy, but the effect of the episode lay in the prominence of the contenders and the forum of their debate. It is readily apparent that considerable attention was drawn to the Indiana divorce laws.

The popular image of Indiana as a center of migratory divorce eventually also found its way into contemporary literature. In 1881 William Dean Howells used an "Indiana divorce" as the basis of plot for his rather melodramatic novel, *A Modern Instance*. Howells was interested in social reforms, and the notoriety of Indiana's divorce situation undoubtedly provided a tempting foundation for a work on the problem of divorce. *A Modern Instance* became one of his more successful publications and drew further attention to Indiana. In it a Boston wife unexpectedly received a "flimsy, shabbily printed country newspaper" from Indiana, containing a brief notice informing her that she was being sued for divorce in "Tecumseh" County. (Copies of the newspaper notices were in fact usually sent to defendants whose whereabouts had been revealed.) The comment of a woman character in the work was probably typical of actual reactions in real life. When the circumstances of the Indiana procedure were explained to her, she remarked, "Oh, it's a cruel, cruel law! . . . To suppose that such a

---

[36] Greeley, 573-578.
[37] *Ibid.*, 578-617. Important sections of the Indiana divorce law effective in 1860 are reprinted on 617-618.

notice as this is sufficient! Women couldn't have made such a law."[38] The plot then followed the events in the wife's legal struggle to protect her name and rights. By the time Howells published his novel, the Indiana law had been changed in several important particulars, and the condemnation of Indiana was no longer really justified. But *A Modern Instance* attests to the national publicity Indiana had attracted during the preceding decades.

From the foregoing presentation it is apparent that Indiana became a center of migratory divorce by a combination of factors. Certainly the state had the right to grant divorces to its *bona fide* residents irrespective of the place of marriage and accrual of cause. Grounds recognized by the state were definitely liberal for the time, but court decisions sustained their permissibility. The method of notice to nonresident defendants was a proper and accepted one in legitimate cases. And divorce decrees once granted could not in terms of practical social realities be opened or voided. Yet the abuses that could occur are well represented in the cases herein selected from the thousands that were filed. To correct the weaknesses of the law and its operation became the task of the legislature after 1852.

Reform Efforts before the Civil War

Although some attempt was made to alter the law of divorce in almost every legislative session, it was virtually impossible to obtain agreement between the houses. Thus, most efforts to change the law failed because the issues involved were not yet of broad concern. An example of this situation was the Senate's passage of a bill in 1853 to give common pleas courts divorce jurisdiction, then limited to circuit courts, and the House's emphatic rejection by a vote of 76 to 0 of similar legislation.[39] And in 1855 the Senate approved an amendment asserting women's rights to their real estate when they secured divorces,[40] but the House took no action. By 1857 the faults of the law had become quite apparent, however, and there was a growing demand for amendment. In presenting an opinion

---

[38] William Dean Howells, *A Modern Instance* (Boston, 1881); the quotations are from the Riverside College Classic Edition, 458, 462.
[39] *Journal of the Senate* (1853), 365, 368, 384; *Journal of the House of Representatives* (1853), 539, 593, 836, 887-888.
[40] *Journal of the Senate* (1855), 205, 219, 242, 253-254.

that year, the Indiana Supreme Court commented that "it is time that legal strictness was adhered to in deciding divorce cases. The facility with which divorces have been granted has proved a curse to the social state."[41] Governor Joseph A. Wright was equally concerned and told the legislature:

> The statute on the subject of granting divorces requires a revision which will relieve our courts from the pressure of applications for divorce, for all imaginable causes, on the part of citizens of other States. You will, doubtless, promptly apply a remedy for this state of things by requiring of the parties, in such cases, an actual residence of two or more years.[42]

But when the legislature considered divorce reform, more emphasis was placed on eliminating "all imaginable causes" than on establishing stronger residence qualifications. In the Senate a bill to alter the residence requirements became the object of general debate. Lewis Wallace proposed amendment of the grounds for divorce to lengthen the period of abandonment by the husband to three years and by the wife to two years, to modify other wording and to drop the discretionary clause that permitted such diversity in causes. He also sought, very unrealistically, postdivorce restrictions. Partners in adultery might never marry under pain of prosecution for "bigamy," and others might not marry for three years. But the Judiciary Committee's amendments were adopted by the Senate. Abandonment of one year's duration by the husband and of two years' time by the wife entitled the spouse to a divorce; the discretionary clause was narrowed to read "any other cause in fraud of the marriage contract, occurring previous to the marriage." Upon final vote the Senate passed the bill 42 to 4, but the House refused to take action on the Senate proposal.[43] Meanwhile the House had passed its own general reform bill concerning residence, causes, alimony, and property issues, but these were substantially less radical in nature than the Senate changes. When the Senate received the House bill, it amended the proposals to embody its own ideas, including elimination of the discretionary clause which the House had left untouched, after which the bill was passed without difficulty. The House rejected the Senate amendments, and the deadlock prevailed until the end of the session.[44]

---

[41] Stoner v. Stoner, 9 Ind. 505 (1857).
[42] *Journal of the House of Representatives* (1857), 34.
[43] *Journal of the Senate* (1857), 81, 90-91, 141-142, 281-283; *Journal of the House of Representatives* (1857), 575, 589, 963.
[44] *Journal of the House of Representatives* (1857), 178, 201-202, 231-232, 837; *Journal of the Senate* (1857), 301-302, 360, 387-388.

In the special legislative session of 1858 Wallace introduced another bill to effect divorce reform. A select committee including Wallace was appointed to consider the entire divorce question, and its composite report suggested broad but rather moderate changes. Principal points in the recommendations were a requirement of residence for one year in the state and six months in the county of suit, retention of the discretionary clause, and modification of various procedural aspects concerning service or notice and subsequent trial. Although there were numerous objections to the several features of these proposals, the bill passed the Senate 47 to 2.[45] A similar pattern was meanwhile being followed in the House, where a special committee on divorce reform also recommended requirement of one year's residence and denial of divorce for desertion of less than a year. Passage of the House bill was obtained by a 90 to 4 vote.[46] Once again the two branches of the legislature could not agree on the changes to be effected, however, and each rejected part of the other's amendments. The Senate was now willing to retain the controversial discretionary clause but insisted on incorporating its other ideas before it passed the House bill; the House merely laid the Senate bill on the table.[47] Yet it was very clear that both bodies were concerned about the divorce problem and that their differences were being reconciled. In particular, there was now agreement on establishment of a year's residence requirement and insistence on proof of abandonment for at least twelve months.

Indicative of the strong demand for reform was that it formed the subject matter of Senate Bill No. 1 in the 1859 legislature. The bill as amended on the floor and in the Judiciary Committee modified six sections of the divorce law. In general it resembled earlier Senate proposals. Specification of a year's residence and proof of a year's minimum desertion remained, the discretionary clause was retained in spite of efforts to repeal it, and provision was made for opening decrees on matters of alimony, property, and child custody. Again the bill easily passed the Senate by a vote of 42 to 3 but was ignored in the House in favor of that body's own legislation.[48] Of the various

[45] *Journal of the Senate* (1858), 30, 36, 80, 84, 162-164; *Brevier Legislative Reports* (1858), first volume called *The Legislative Sentinel*, 25, 54, 100-101.

[46] *Journal of the House of Representatives* (1858), 31, 65-66, 150-152, 183-184; *Brevier Legislative Reports* (1858), 30, 52, 110-111, 118.

[47] *Journal of the Senate* (1858), 192, 197, 205, 301-306; *Journal of the House of Representatives* (1858), 200, 237; *Brevier Legislative Reports* (1858), 126, 133, 178.

[48] *Journal of the Senate* (1859), 41-42, 157-159, 209-211, 250, 253-254; *Brevier Legislative Reports* (1859), 20, 74-75; *Journal of the House of Representatives* (1859), 267, 431, 502-503.

divorce reform bills introduced in the House, favor was shown to Bill No. 93 to affect the residence and abandonment sections. After the bill passed the House by 75 to 2 votes, the Judiciary Committee stated that "further legislation is inexpedient" and asked to be relieved of consideration of divorce bills.[49] The House bill was subsequently amended in the Senate, but the House accepted most of the Senate changes. It did refuse to allow the Senate's proposal to permit opening of divorce decrees even for limited purposes, and objected to some other points as well, so that a committee of free conference had to be established to resolve the differences. Most basic points advocated by the Senate were ultimately accepted, with tighter wording, and both the Senate and House passed the compromise version of the House bill.[50]

Analysis of the amendments contained in the law of March 4, 1859, shows that the changes were quite moderate.[51] To discourage migratory divorces the new law imposed a requirement of one year's residence in the state and current residence in the county of filing. The petitioner's own affidavit would no longer constitute *prima facie* evidence of residence, but proof of residence would have to be offered to the court's satisfaction. These changes were prompted by the recognized fact that "advantage is daily taken of the existing law by non-resident parties, who are not entitled to a divorce," and the changes therefore took effect immediately. Only one modification was made in the grounds for divorce: abandonment had to be at least one year in duration. A longer interval between service and trial was provided by the stipulation that required personal service ten days and publication notice thirty days before the first day of the court term. The 1852 law had merely demanded fourteen or thirty days, respectively, before the case could be heard and determined. Section 14 of the original law had declared that "The defendant may in addition to his or her answer file a cross petition for divorce, and the court shall in such case decree the divorce, if any, in favor of the party legally entitled to the same."[52] Court interpretation of this provision had thereafter created much controversy. In 1850 the Indiana Supreme Court had ruled in a nondivorce case that "an original

---

[49] *Journal of the House of Representatives* (1859), 135, 166, 410, 586, 669, 732 (quotation), for miscellaneous bills, and 149, 170, 409-410, 491, for principal bill.
[50] *Journal of the Senate* (1859), 485-486, 506-509, 694, 790, 837-838, 963-964; *Journal of the House of Representatives* (1859), 739-740, 851-852, 873, 961, 998-999, 1056; *Brevier Legislative Reports* (1859), 180, 238, 243, 288-289.
[51] *Laws of the State of Indiana, Passed at the Fortieth Regular Session of the General Assembly, 1859* (Indianapolis, 1859), 108-110.
[52] *The Statutes of 1852*, Gavin and Hord Edition, II, 348-354.

22

and a cross-bill make but one suit," and dismissal of the original petition threw the entire matter out of court. Trial could not proceed on the cross-petition because it was only a dependency of the principal bill.[53] The court was forced to rule in a divorce case in 1857 and affirmed its earlier decision. Only when both petitions were still before the trial court was Section 14 held to be applicable, for dismissal of the original petition made a divorce on the cross-petition impossible.[54] The 1859 amendments specifically allowed the case to continue in court after dismissal of the original petition and declared that no further notice of the pendency of the case was necessary under such circumstances. All the foregoing changes in the 1852 law were enacted without much objection.

There was considerable disagreement over the question of permitting defendants to open divorce decrees after they were granted. Inherent in the proposal was recognition that the existing procedures often proved unjust to absent and innocent defendants. The Senate appeared willing to allow divorce judgments to be opened and presumably voided within two years unless a party had meanwhile remarried. But some senators opposed the idea "because it would have the effect of an advertisement, inviting foreigners into this State for the purposes of opening up old cases." Another senator commented that everyone who spoke in favor of the suggestion "seems to think that this law has been a disgrace to our State." The position of the state courts on this issue, previously discussed, was for reasons of public policy against opening cases. Moreover, the House was adamantly opposed to such action.[55] But certain hardships were acknowledged by the 1859 amendment law. It declared that where only newspaper notice was used a defendant in any earlier or subsequent case might open the judgment at any time as to the care, support, or custody of children.[56] And in cases decided after March, 1859, defendants who were only constructively notified by publication could reopen the cases within two years concerning alimony and property settlements, but property sold to *bona fide* purchasers could not be affected. In no instance could the actual dissolution of the

---

[53] Elderkin v. Fitch, 2 Ind. 90 (1850).
[54] Stoner v. Stoner, 9 Ind. 505 (1857). In a case earlier the same year on such an issue, Stafford v. Stafford, 9 Ind. 162 (1857), the court had not ruled because of unclear evidence.
[55] *Journal of the Senate* (1859), 506-509; *Brevier Legislative Reports* (1859), 74-75 (quotations); and *Journal of the House of Representatives* (1859), 998-999.
[56] There is no accurate statistical data on the problem of children in divorce cases for this general period. About half the Indiana divorce cases reported the existence of children, but no information concerning children was recorded in most instances. *Marriage and Divorce, 1867-1906*, part II, 662.

marriage contract be set aside, however, and the 1859 law thus stated emphatically what the Supreme Court had long held on judicial principle.

Alimony created no grave problems a century ago. The 1852 law had allowed courts to decree alimony, and the 1859 changes merely simplified the phraseology employed. In general, alimony was determined by what the court deemed just and proper in each divorce case. Since the law required that alimony could only be decreed for a sum in gross, periodic payments could not be awarded because the total amount would be indeterminate, although a husband was allowed to pay the stipulated full sum in separate installments. Only cash was authorized as alimony. In 1855 the state Supreme Court had held it to be error when a court awarded property as alimony to a wife.[57] Other changes in the law gave wives greater protection in respect to their own property in divorce cases and reflected the growing sentiment in favor of women's rights and independence in legal affairs. But such issues accounted for little objection in the general divorce reform movement.

After the enactment of the 1859 amendments, and with the outbreak of the Civil War, the divorce question receded into the background. Although there was general satisfaction with the 1859 reforms, a few efforts to secure further changes were made, but they failed to gain much support. An attempt was made in the House in the regular session of 1861 to tighten the law by further amendment of Section 6 to prevent persons from other states from "coming here and obtaining a residence on their own affidavit," as still often occurred. The bill almost passed but was recommitted and died in committee.[58] When an attempt was made to authorize suits for alimony in the same session, the House Judiciary Committee expressed the view that further legislation on the subject was not then warranted.[59] As might be expected, there was no discussion of divorce in the special session of the General Assembly in the spring of 1861. A further effort to stiffen divorce procedures nearly passed in 1863 when a House bill requiring prosecuting attorneys of common pleas courts to appear and defend in divorce cases where the defendant was absent failed in the Senate by only one vote.[60] But

---

[57] *Statutes of 1852*, Gavin and Hord Edition, II, 348-354, Sections 19 and 22; Green v. Green, 7 Ind. 113 (1855).
[58] *Journal of the House of Representatives* (1861), 174, 309, 359, 746-747, 1043-1044; *Brevier Legislative Reports* (1861), 173, 326 (quotation).
[59] *Journal of the House of Representatives* (1861), 304, 483.
[60] *Journal of the House of Representatives* (1863), 63, 91, 198-199, 300-301; *Journal of the Senate* (1863), 254-255, 271, 357, 419-420; *Brevier Legislative Reports* (1863), 46, 115, 158.

attempts to alter residence requirements and repeal all grounds but adultery were unsuccessful.[61]

The Divorce Law of 1873

In spite of more pressing problems arising from termination of the Civil War, considerable attention was given to divorce reform in 1865. The Senate passed two bills in the regular legislative session and one in the special session to effect changes in divorce procedures. One of its bills required two years' actual residence in the state, verified by affidavits of two householders, but the House never brought the bill to a vote.[62] In the special session late in 1865 the Senate attempted to prescribe the terms on which divorces could be granted where the cause accrued out of the state.[63] Again the bill was allowed to die in the House. The third Senate bill corrected a situation that could not be ignored, however, and eventually was enacted to amend Section 349 of the 1852 Practice Act. It was introduced by Senator George S. Brown of Adams, Jay, and Wells counties, and his own explanation of the procedural problem is most valuable:

> This bill is intended to put an end to the fraudulent procurement of divorces in Indiana by non-resident parties. . . . Agencies are established in New York and other Eastern cities, which advertise to procure divorces for any parties desiring the same, whether cause therefor exist or not. These agencies have lawyers in this State to whom they send the cases, at the same time forging the name of the defendant to a written retainer, which, with a fee, they send to another attorney, in the entire confidence of the thing. These two attorneys enter our courts, procure the referment of the case to a third attorney, also in the confidence of the matter, who has his fee in the case, and who reports in favor of a divorce without ever receiving or examining any evidence in the case whatever. All this proceeding is fraudulently procured by these divorce agencies. Upon this report of the referee, it would seem, the courts have no discretion but to grant the divorce. Thus hundreds of divorces have been heretofore procured in the courts of this State annually by non-residents, and in no case have the defendants probably been aware of the fact until long after the same are procured.

[61] *Journal of the House of Representatives* (1863), 133, 189, 369, 461; *Journal of the Senate* (1863), 590-591, 631; *Brevier Legislative Reports* (1863), 68, 199.
[62] *Journal of the Senate* (1865), 186, 223, 345, 395; *Brevier Legislative Reports* (1865), 129; *Journal of the House of Representatives* (1865), 532; *Journal of the House of Representatives, Called Session* (1865), 156, 600; *Brevier Legislative Reports, Extra Session* (1865), 235.
[63] *Journal of the Senate, Called Session* (1865), 233, 255, 267-268, 311; *Brevier Legislative Reports, Extra Session* (1865), 132, 147, 159.

Following Brown's comments the Senate passed unanimously his amendment to prevent such referral of divorce cases.[64] In the House the proposal was approved after Representative H. C. Newcomb of Marion County stated that "from conversation with members from the northeast part of the State, he found these statements fully sustained."[65] Others also admitted the prevalence of the referral custom in Wells County but attributed its existence to the actions of a few individuals. The situation furnishes an interesting example, however, of how Indiana divorces could be obtained. Except for elimination of the flagrant abuse by referral to referees, the House showed much less interest in divorce reform than the Senate in 1865.[66]

With the higher divorce rate in the years after the Civil War and the continued existence of evasive practices, the demand for fundamental revision of the divorce law grew steadily in strength. The major effort in 1867 centered on a surprisingly strict Senate bill introduced by Firman Church of Lake, Porter, and Newton counties that required among other provisions five years' residence where grievances cited occurred outside the state, specific affidavits concerning the couple's last residence and the petitioner's knowledge of the defendant's whereabouts, and repeal of the discretionary clause. On the floor of the Senate the bill occasioned a dispute on the entire divorce question. The comparative severity of the bill was firmly pressed by Church, who condemned the leniency of the existing system that encouraged migratory decrees: "Ninety-nine out of one hundred divorces obtained in this State would never be granted if the defendants knew of their pendancy and could get here to make their plea." But the very strictness of his solution doomed the proposal. One senator branded the bill "An act to prevent divorces in the State of Indiana," and after a series of close votes on amendment and procedure the entire matter lapsed when the Senate adjourned.[67] Thus, even the Senate in 1867 failed to pass any amendatory bill, and the House once more showed still less anxiety over divorce questions.[68]

---

[64] *Journal of the Senate* (1865), 36, 47, 104, 140, 154-155; *Brevier Legislative Reports* (1865), 34, 110 (quotation).
[65] *Journal of the House of Representatives* (1865), 182, 274, 478; *Brevier Legislative Reports* (1865), 287; *Journal of the House of Representatives, Called Session* (1865), 159-161; *Brevier Legislative Reports, Extra Session* (1865), 87-88 (quotation), 90; *Journal of the Senate, Called Session* (1865), 141, 189.
[66] *Journal of the House of Representatives, Called Session* (1865), 223, 429; *Brevier Legislative Reports, Extra Session* (1865), 113, 188-189.
[67] *Journal of the Senate* (1867), 292, 370, 386, 459-460, 722-724; *Brevier Legislative Reports* (1867), 153-154, 191, 231 (quotations), 367.
[68] *Journal of the House of Representatives* (1867), 150, 224-225, 473, 549, 720, 817-818; *Brevier Legislative Reports* (1867), 112, 200.

After a decade of difficulty under the ineffective amendments of 1859, most observers were eager to improve Indiana's poor reputation in respect to divorces. But at the very time that demand for legislative action reached a height, the General Assembly found itself plagued with more critical political problems. As a result, divorce reform was accepted as necessary but less imperative than other issues. None of the bills introduced in the regular session of 1869 received much attention before adjournment,[69] and in the special session two complementary Senate bills to regulate residence and service and to punish petitioners guilty of fraud died in the House.[70] But a House proposal to amend the residence, service, and grounds provisions of the law received the firm endorsement of a Special Committee on divorce:

> Your Committee believing some legislation necessary on the subject of divorces in order that the character of our State may be cleansed from the odium now attached to it on account of its laws in relation to granting divorces, and also that the marriage relation may be rendered in some measure more secure against the inroads of avarice, perfidy and brutality, beg leave to return the bill under consideration, and recommend its passage.

When the bill was taken up in the House, it brought a long speech by Gilbert A. Pierce of Porter County in which he advocated reform to provide against "the disgraceful custom which now permits non-residents to gain a technical residence here for the notorious and avowed purpose of securing a divorce."[71] But any chance of securing changes in the law in 1869 disappeared when the Democratic representatives resigned during the Fifteenth Amendment ratification controversy.

By 1871 the reputation of Indiana as a jurisdiction of easy divorce had become so objectionable that Governor Conrad Baker devoted a long section of his message to the legislature on January 6 to the divorce reform question. He began his remarks with the observation that "the laws of this State regulating the granting of divorces, and especially the lax manner in which they have been administered in some of our courts, has given Indiana a notoriety that is by no means enviable." Baker felt that a "candid review" of

---

[69] *Journal of the Senate* (1869), 85, 191, 364, 694; *Journal of the House of Representatives* (1869), 461, 480, 949.

[70] *Journal of the Senate, Special Session* (1869), 54, 72, 107-108, 188, 190-191; *Journal of the House of Representatives, Special Session* (1869), 270, 305, 563-567; *Brevier Legislative Reports, Special Session* (1869), 53, 112, 217-218.

[71] *Journal of the House of Representatives, Special Session* (1869), 178, 516 (first quotation), 563-567; *Brevier Legislative Reports, Special Session* (1869), 203, 217-218, 228-232 (Pierce's speech with quotation on 232).

27

the subject would "satisfy any impartial mind" that reform was necessary. The governor did not object to any of the specific grounds for divorce, except perhaps the too liberal construction of "cruel treatment" by the courts, but he disliked the lack of uniformity permitted by the law. "Under this discretionary clause causes of divorce vary in the several judicial circuits and districts, with the diversified mental and moral peculiarities of the judges." And he found the practices in divorce proceedings worse than the law itself:

> The facility with which citizens of other States, after a pretended residence in this, can and do procure divorces in our courts, and then return to their homes from which they fled for that very purpose, is a reproach to the civilization of the age, and a breach of that comity which should be scrupulously observed between sister States of the same great republican family.

He found also that Indiana's residence requirement might prove a blessing to others but was "not calculated to give citizens of Indiana a very exalted idea of the righteousness or wisdom of the legislation of their own State." The governor recommended seven specific changes in the law and its administration: (1) repeal the discretionary clause, (2) change the expression "cruel treatment" to "cruel and inhuman" or "cruel and barbarous" treatment, (3) require resident defendants to be sued in the county of their residence, (4) require plaintiffs to be residents for one year before filing and also during the pendency and trial of their causes, (5) limit divorce jurisdiction to circuit courts exclusively, (6) require petitions to show the place where the cause happened or accrued, where the applicant resided at the time, and whether the jurisdiction where the cause accrued would recognize the ground as sufficient for divorce, and (7) require the preceding items to be verified by affidavits accompanying the petition and to be proved during the trial.

> With such amendments as these we might well hope that Indiana divorces would soon cease to be advertised in any of the Atlantic cities as marketable commodities, and that refugees and fugitives from the justice of other States would no longer come to Indiana in quest of divorces to be used on their return as licenses to violate the laws of our sister States.[72]

Two years later Baker also suggested that local prosecuting and district attorneys should report periodically to the Attorney General on divorces granted and refused in their jurisdictions.[73]

---

[72] *Brevier Legislative Reports* (1871), 43-45.
[73] *Ibid.* (1873), appendix, 7.

Popular demand for divorce reform was also growing. Numerous memorials and petitions were sent to the legislature from various counties and groups, asking typically for "repeal of the most objectionable features of our divorce laws, and the enactment of such amendments as will guard their administration against corruption and fraud." A petition drawn up at the annual meeting of the Society of Friends noted that some of Indiana's statutory grounds "actually *encourage* divorce, by offering it as a premium for crime" and that "so much shameful fraud and corruption have characterized the administration of our divorce laws, and many innocent persons have been so cruelly wronged thereby, that great odium attaches to our otherwise fair record and reputation as a State."[74] Out-of-state press commentary also continued to be unfavorable, which prompted one Senator to remark that "in view of the fact that the papers of the United States hold us up to scorn and our own press cannot successfully deny it," reform was absolutely mandatory.[75] Public and press opinion undoubtedly was both responsible for and encouraged by the governor's message. But two years were to pass before the legislature could agree on action.

The Senate once more proved willing to effect reforms and passed a divorce bill that met the governor's request. It required one year's residence in the state and county under normal circumstances but two years' residence if the ground arose when the parties were not Indiana residents. In respect to causes for divorce, it denied the remedy of divorce until three years after the marriage except for adultery and infamous crime, and it dropped the discretionary clause entirely. An attempt was also made to allow publication notice only where the defendant's whereabouts were completely unknown.[76] Several bills of varying nature were presented in the House. The Committee on Rights and Privileges reported that, in response to "petitions of various citizens of the State of Indiana, in regard to the divorce laws," it had examined the problem and felt that with repeal of the discretionary clause "the present law on the subject will be unexceptionable, and will compare favorably with that of any other State." But the Judiciary Committee, after consideration of the Senate bill and the House proposals, presented its own sub-

---

[74] *Journal of the Senate* (1871), 397-398 (first quotation); *Brevier Legislative Reports* (1871), 85 (second quotation), 201, 214, 335; the Friends resubmitted their petition in 1872, *Brevier Legislative Reports* (1872), 86; see also W. S. Haymond, *An Illustrated History of the State of Indiana* (Indianapolis, 1879), 252.
[75] *Brevier Legislative Reports* (1873), 454.
[76] *Journal of the Senate* (1871), 73-74, 138, 424-426; *Brevier Legislative Reports* (1871), 53, 204.

stitute bill. Residence was set at two years and the discretionary clause was repealed.[77] Again adjournment came before the House took any vote, however, and reform was once more postponed.

When the special session of the legislature met in November, 1872, divorce reform was regarded as virtually inevitable. Several bills were introduced in each house during the prolonged deliberations that continued in the subsequent regular session of 1873. Residence requirements and grounds for divorce were naturally the main subject matter.[78] In the House attention was focused on Bill No. 333 advanced by Thomas W. Woollen of Johnson County. From his work on the Judiciary Committee, Woollen was able to devise a bill embodying the essential reform demands. In discussion of the bill on the floor of the House, Woollen acknowledged that the reform might hurt his own and others' legal practices, but he added that "public sentiment for at least ten years has demanded these changes in this law. Honest men have had it thrown into their faces, that the divorce laws of Indiana were a disgrace; and that is the public sentiment outside as well [as] inside of the State." The bill was passed 56 to 21 by the House on January 28, 1873, after a minimum of debate.[79] In the Senate action came more slowly. Bill No. 117 proposed by James Orr of Delaware and Madison counties, who desired "to wipe out the reproach now resting upon the State because of our loose divorce laws," was selected to become the reform measure, but its path through the Senate was not smooth and Orr fought to keep it alive. Later the Committee on Rights and Privileges practically rewrote it to include various viewpoints. Although Orr was not entirely happy with the rewritten bill, he supported it as an improvement over existing legislation. It was passed in the Senate by 30 to 15 votes on February 25.[80] Since the Senate bill was deliberately made quite similar to the one already passed by the House, the Senate took no action on the House bill. But Woollen was instrumental in guiding the Senate bill through the House to final

[77] *Journal of the House of Representatives* (1871), 85, 93, 160-161, 183, 218, 476, 508-509, 885-886 (quotation), 902-904; *Brevier Legislative Reports* (1871), 55, 60, 80, 109, 219, 336.

[78] *Journal of the Senate* (1872), 44, 79, 153, 360, 552; *Journal of the House of Representatives* (1872), 74, 76, 97, 119, 221; *Brevier Legislative Reports* (1872), 51, 143, 267; *Journal of the Senate* (1873), 137-138, 269-270, 311, 548, 765, 799, 835, 978; *Journal of the House of Representatives* (1873), 132-133, 165, 524.

[79] *Journal of the House of Representatives* (1873), 135, 163-164, 233, 247; *Brevier Legislative Reports* (1873), 57, 88, 90 (continued on 376-382; quotation on 376).

[80] *Journal of the Senate* (1872), 201; *Brevier Legislative Reports* (1872), 160; *Journal of the Senate* (1873), 134, 154, 264-269, 481-484, 670-671; *Brevier Legislative Reports* (1873), 59 (quotation; debate continued on 335-337), 63, 87-88, 146-147 (continued on 453-455), 202.

passage on March 6 by a vote of 69 to 29. Four days later the new divorce law became effective.[81]

The divorce law of 1873 was designed only to correct the worst features of the earlier statute. Hence, it was not fundamentally different in most respects from the amended law of 1852.[82] Since its purpose was the prevention of easy divorce in Indiana by residents or others, the residence and grounds portions were most altered, with other sections changed only slightly. Divorces were still allowed for seven causes under Section 8 of the new law, but the causes most frequently abused were changed. The discretionary clause was dropped entirely, and abandonment was raised from one to two years' duration. Residence requirements were similarly stiffened. Under the 1873 statute a residence of two years in the state and six months in the county of suit was stipulated, and proof by affidavit of two resident freeholders and householders was demanded. Details of past residence were required to prevent fraud. Provision for opening of divorce decrees was retained in a tighter fashion. Where only publication notice was obtained, past or future decrees could be opened at any time as to care, support, and custody of children; subsequent divorces could be opened within two years as to the decree itself, alimony, and property settlement. Those who secured such divorces consequently might not remarry within two years of the decree.

Effects of Reform

With the changes in the law it was assumed, as the governor and others wished, that Indiana would cease to be a haven for divorce-seekers. The new provisions certainly did not seriously hamper legitimate residents who petitioned for divorces.[83] Table II shows that there were actually more decrees granted after 1873 in Indiana than before the new law was passed. A growing population and an increasing acceptance of divorce in society undoubtedly account for

---

[81] *Journal of the Senate* (1873), 799, 978; *Journal of the House of Representatives* (1873), 609-610, 688, 724, 806, 811-813, 899, 902, 917; *Brevier Legislative Reports* (1873), 245 (reporting passage vote as 69 to 23).
[82] The text of the 1873 law may be found in *Laws of the State of Indiana, Passed at the Forty-Eighth Regular Session of the General Assembly, 1873* (Indianapolis, 1873), 107-112, and in *The Statutes of the State of Indiana: Containing the Revised Statutes of 1852, with the Amendments Thereto, and the Subsequent Legislation* (Indianapolis, 1876), edited by Edwin A. Davis, II, 324-332.
[83] See William S. Garber, "Divorce in Marion County," *The Indiana Magazine of History*, VI, no. 1 (March, 1910), 1-16.

the higher figures. But Indiana no longer was sought out by those from other states seeking quick and easy divorce, and criticism of the state therefore ceased with the usage of the new statute. Perhaps the situation is best summarized by the wife's father in Howells' *A Modern Instance*, written after the 1873 law became effective, when he commented that his son-in-law "must have been disappointed when he found a divorce so hard to get in Indiana."[84]

It is now easy to see that the entire divorce issue in Indiana a hundred years ago grew beyond normal proportion by a combination of circumstantial factors. Divorce reform necessarily involved such controversial questions as lax judicial practices, religious concepts, women's rights, humanitarianism, and temperance; and the great diversity of views held and expressed on such topics prevented easy agreement on solutions. Official preoccupation with problems of the Civil War and Reconstruction prolonged unfortunately the life of a divorce law that admittedly permitted unscrupulous individuals to take advantage of the state's courts. The modification of the statutory provisions was thus an almost inevitable reaction to an embarrassing situation. But much of what was deemed exceptionable concerning divorce a century ago has long since become accepted practice in the United States. And when the concern of nineteenth-century critics of liberal divorce is viewed in present-day perspective, the concluding judgment of one Indiana legislator in 1873 on the whole divorce question in the preceding decades appears even more valid: "We have been a little in advance of the age, instead of being a little behind."[85]

---

[84] Howells, 462-463.
[85] *Brevier Legislative Reports* (1873), 378.

94